Nathan Levy's

STORIES WITH HOLES
VOLUME 6
Revised & Updated
By Nathan Levy

A collection of original thinking
activities for improving inquiry!

An N.L. Associates, Inc. book

N.L. Associates, Inc.
PO Box 1199
Hightstown, NJ 08520-0399

Library of Congress Catalog Number
89-92195
ISBN 1-878347-63-2

Copyright © 2005 N.L. Associates, Inc.

Printed in the United States of America

i

PREFACE – by Nathan Levy

This book is the result of several years' accumulation of ideas leading to puzzling stories that lend themselves to what I call thinking games. The "games" have become the means for thousands of people to carry on a totally enjoyable process of engaging critical and imaginative thinking. Volume 1 of my Stories with Holes is a collection of stories that has been gathered from various sources. Nathan Levy's Stories with Holes Volumes 2-20 are original. Wherever I speak I share some of the stories with my training groups. Teachers, parents and children enjoy the stories immensely. I hope you will as well.

INTRODUCTION

The objectives of using Nathan Levy's Stories with Holes include the following:

- to provide for growth in imagination and intuitive functioning
- to give experiences that display the fun of working cooperatively, rather than competitively, on a common problem
- to increase cognitive skills of resolving discrepancies through successful experiences
- to provide enjoyable changes-of-pace for task-oriented learning environments

This is a structured activity. It is designed to ensure involvement on the part of each participant, and to promote feelings of group and individual success.

The games are designed to accommodate all levels. "Children" from ages 8-88 will benefit from using these stories.

The time a story takes will vary. Usually a story lasts from 3 to 30 minutes, but some stories can take days. Children, lower grades through high school, tend to regard these thinking games as play instead of work. It is one of the few activities I know of that "hooks" almost anyone into creative use of their intelligence, i.e. learning, almost in spite of themselves. Nathan Levy's Stories with Holes are for all groups over age seven, regardless of background or achievement level.

**Please note that I have revised the above introduction and the following methodology from the way they appeared in the original collection of Stories with Holes. The revisions are based on my current workshop experiences with children and adults.

N.L.

iii

METHODOLOGY

The first time a group plays, it will be necessary to begin by announcing something like the following: "I am going to tell you a story with a hole in it – I mean that an important part of the story is missing. Listen carefully so you can find the missing part, for the story may not seem to make much sense to you at first..."

At this point, tell the story once, pause, and then tell it the same way again. Then say...

"You can ask questions that can be answered either with a "yes" or with a "no". I can only answer "yes", "no", "does not compute", or "is not relevant". If I answer, "does not compute", that means that the question you asked cannot receive a straight "yes" or "no" without throwing you off the track."

Allow for questions about the process, if there are any, but usually it is best simply to jump into the game by having the questioning start. The process becomes clear as the game progresses. Once a group has played the game, the full directions given above for playing the game are unnecessary.

From this point on, answer only in one of the four designated ways. The following is an example of a computed story taken from Stories with Holes, and how it might be played:

Story: Mitch lives on the twentieth floor of an apartment building. Every time he leaves, he rides a self-service elevator from the twentieth floor to the street; but every time he returns, he rides the same self-service elevator only to the fifteenth floor, where he leaves the elevator and walks up the remaining five flights of stairs. Repeat, then ask who knows the answer already; if any do, ask them to observe and not give away the answer.

Question: Does the elevator go all the way up?
Answer: Yes.
Q: Does he want the exercise?
A: No.
Q: Does it have something to do with the elevator not working right?
A: No.
Q: Does he have a girlfriend on the 15th floor who he stops to see?
A: No.
Q: Does he have something different about him?
A: Yes.
Q: Is he a robber?
A: No.
Q: Is he a real person?
A: Yes.
Q: A tall person?
A: No.
Q: Is his size important?
A: Yes.
Q: I know! He's too short to reach the button!
A: Right!

v

At this point, make certain that all the participants understand the answer and why it is the correct answer. In the example given above, the group found the answer quite soon. Instead of starting a new game -- particularly if this is the first time playing – spend some time processing the game with questions like:

* What did you have to do in order to play this game? (Listen, hear each answer, think, imagine, follow a line of reasoning, eliminate possibilities, etc.)

* Ask the person who finally solved the riddle, "Joanne, did you have help from others in finding the answer?" It nearly always comes out that the person relied on previous questions and answers. Use this to point out the interdependence of players, and reduce competition within the group to be the "winner".

* When do you see yourself having to use the kind of thinking you use in this game?

Usually a group of youngsters will be eager to try a second game right away.

Some important points to remember:

1. Immediately following the telling of each story and before the questioning begins, ask if anyone in the group has heard it before and knows the answer. Tell these people to observe and refrain from questioning.

2. Use the "does not compute" response whenever a single word or phrase in a question makes it impossible to answer with a "yes" or "no" answer. Examples from the story above:

- "Why does he live on the twentieth floor?" "Why" questions, as well as "where, who, when or which", cannot be answered "yes" or "no".

- "Does the elevator operator make him get off at the fifteenth floor?" No mention was made of an operator.

3. If a game goes past 10 or 12 minutes and some people begin to lose interest close the game for the present. There is absolutely nothing harmful in leaving the puzzle unsolved. The group can return to it another time, when interest and energy are high. Some students may protest, but do not give the answer. The experience of non-closure provides some valuable learning in itself; but more importantly, once a group has expended considerable energy on the game, the victory should be an earned one. Although there may be some unusual circumstances under which you would give the group the answer, I have found it best not to do so (even if some are begging). The point here is not to "take the answer away by giving it." You can always return to it later. What is important is that the students earn the feeling of "we-did-it!"

4. Share the computer (leader) role. Once kids have learned how the game works, have a volunteer lead the game. He or she must choose from the stories he

or she already knows. As soon as you are convinced the student is familiar with the story, the answer, and the process (which you should previously have modeled) have the leader read the story to the class, and begin taking questions. Most important here is what you model. A child-led computer game is an excellent small-group activity to have going on while you are occupied elsewhere in the classroom.

5. You may periodically want to encourage categorical thinking. When a player asks a question beginning, "Would it help us to know..." or "Does it have anything to do with..." pause in the game and show how the type of question is uniquely helpful in narrowing down the range of questions, distilling and focusing the group's attention, or cutting away large slices of the topic that are irrelevant. Thus, the question "Is David's occupation important?" tends to be more useful than "Is he a plumber? A teacher?", etc.

6. Be sure that a question is exactly true, or exactly false, before responding. One word can make the difference.

1. The Space Shuttle

The Space Shuttle flew up in the air, then tumbled end over end to earth, landing without damage.

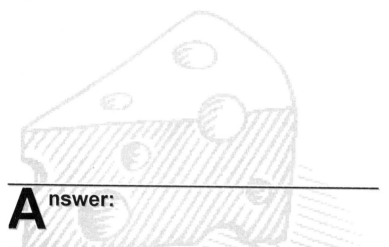

Answer:

The Space Shuttle was a balsa wood rocket.

2. The Sword

Al leaped forward with his sword high. Yet he was defenseless.

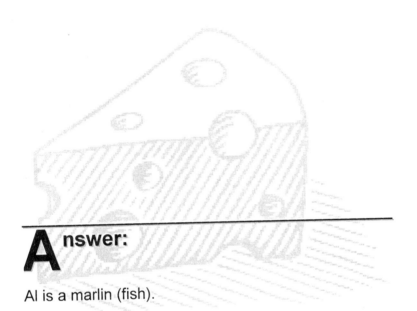

Answer:

Al is a marlin (fish).

3. The Eagle

Scott Hobson was overjoyed when he shot an eagle. Three policemen observed the shot yet nothing was done to Scott.

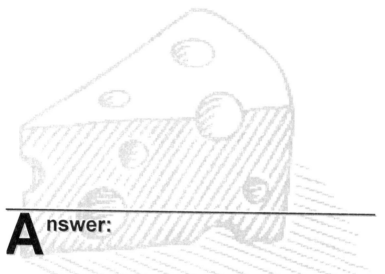

Answer:

Scott made two under par on a golf hole. (3 strokes on a par 5, 2 on a par 4.)

4. Lives Lost

Many lives were lost on Arizona land. The location is memorialized – as it should have been.

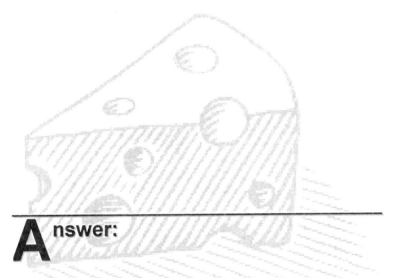

Answer:

The Arizona was a famous battleship at Pearl Harbor which was attacked on December 7, 1941.

5. The Rings

Terry and Mike took four priceless rings. Terry retired and Mike went for more. The police knew who both men were and where they were, but they left Terry and Mike alone. Why?

Answer:

Terry Bradshaw and Mike Webster both played for the Pittsburgh Steelers and won four Super Bowls. Terry retired and Mike kept on playing.

6. A Popped Cork

The cork popped, the liquid flowed, but ten minutes later Lynda and Karen suffered greatly.

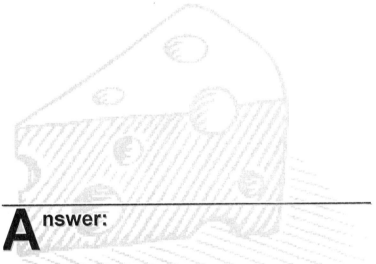

Answer:

A boat cork popped, water rushed in and Lynda and Karen went into the icy water.

7. A Magic Container

The container would not hold the material, but if the product was bigger it would hold more. The contents of the box kept shrinking, getting smaller and smaller, yet not disappearing for a long time.

Answer:

The box was a square glass with a hole in it. The contents, liquid, kept "shrinking" by leaking out. Small "puddles" always remained for a while.

8. The Case of the Female Strangler

Hundreds of detectives were baffled by the case of the female strangler. Detective Frank Gross had inside information that could definitely lead to the capture of this dangerous criminal.

A **nswer:**

Frank Gross was the female strangler.

9. The Bouncing Ball

The ball fell deeply into the hole and did not bounce out, but it never went beneath the ground.

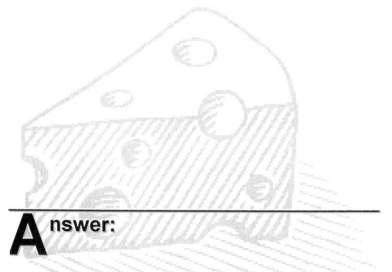

Answer:

The hole was between center field and right field in a baseball game.

10. The Drowning Man

Gary Yepez was drowning. When they rescued Gary he was not wet.

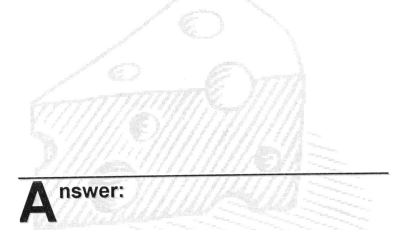

Answer:

Gary had pneumonia. The fluid on his lungs was drowning him until the doctors helped to relieve the problem.

11. A Hit on the Head

The hit on Isaac's head changed things in the open field.

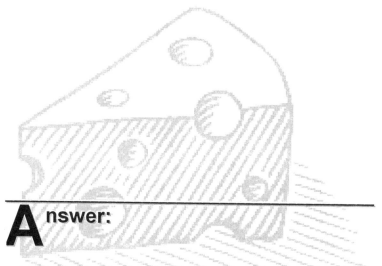

Answer:

An empty field was now covered with apples that had fallen from the tree.

12. In the Dark

As Jason entered the dark room the light went on. Jason had touched nothing, there were no light switches or lamps in the room, nor was an automatic timer used. What created the illumination?

Answer:

There was central lighting and it was turned on from another room.

12

13. The Singer

Little Kimberly was singing, "Daylight coming, I want to go home." Why that song?

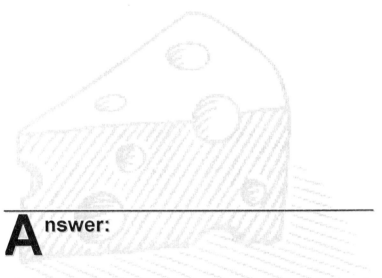

Answer:

Kimberly was a vampire who wanted to get home to her coffin before daylight.

14. A Ship's Steward

Angie, the ship's steward, knew she had to deliver fresh coffee in a fine cup and saucer to V.M. Neal, the gangster, one level up. The ship started to sway in heavy seas. Angie's health depended on the coffee being delivered in the porcelain cup – heavy seas were no excuse to V.M.

Answer:

Angie put the coffee in her mouth until she got to the side of V.M.'s room. Then Angie spit the coffee back into the gangster's cup and served him.

14

15. The Torn Earrings

The earrings were savagely ripped from Margaret's ears by the violent thief. Though a little shaken, Margaret experienced no pain or damage to either ear.

Answer:

Margaret wore clip-on earrings.

15

16. The Roamer

Dominique could only be seen at night as she roamed the halls of the huge castle. Many people came to visit daily – never seeing Dominique.

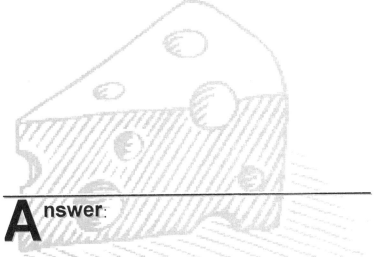

A nswer:

Dominique was the night janitor of the tourist attraction and she slept days.

17. A Family Member

If Jack H. is a very important part of a family, why is he so often thrown around?

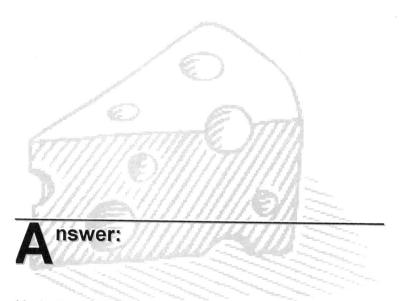

A **nswer:**

He is the Jack of Hearts in a deck of cards.

17

18. A Harmful Drink

Stephanie McCartney drank the tee and had to receive medical treatment immediately.

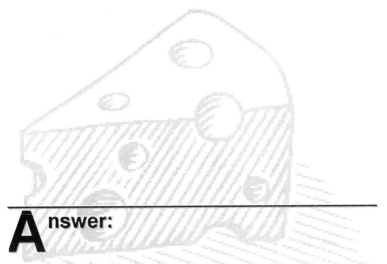

Answer:

Stephanie's drink contained a golf tee, which lodged in her throat.

18

19. The Bear in Motion

The bear could only move in a circle. Scientists constantly examined the bear's motions, but never did anything to help.

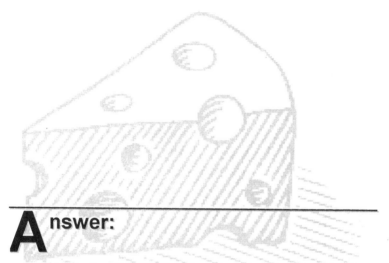

Answer:

The bear is the Bear Constellation.

19

20. The Ice Cream Sisters

Denise went to the ice cream shop with her sister, Jane. They both got ice cream although they ordered only one cone.

Answer:

Denise ate half of Jane's cone.

Nathan Levy

Nathan Levy is the author of more than 40 books which have sold almost 250,000 copies to teachers and parents in the US, Europe, Asia, South America, Australia and Africa. His unique <u>Stories with Holes</u> series continues to be proclaimed the most popular activity used in gifted, special education and regular classrooms by hundreds of educators. An extremely popular, dynamic speaker on thinking, writing and differentiation, Nathan is in high demand as a workshop leader in school and business settings. As a former school principal, company president, parent of four daughters and management trainer, Nathan's ability to transfer knowledge and strategies to audiences through humorous, thought provoking stories assures that participants leave with a plethora of new ways to approach their future endeavors.

NL Associates is pleased to be the publisher of this book. Teachers, students and other readers are invited to contribute their own "Stories with Holes" for possible inclusion in future volumes. Suggested stories will not be returned to you and will be acknowledged only if selected. Please send your suggestions to:

NL Associates Inc
PO Box 1199
Hightstown NJ 08520-0399
www.storieswithholes.com

Dynamic Speakers
Creative Workshops
Relevant Topics

Nathan Levy, author of the <u>Stories with Holes</u> series and <u>There Are Those</u>, and other nationally known authors and speakers, can help your school or organization achieve positive results with children. We can work with you to provide a complete in-service package or have one of our presenters lead one of several informative and entertaining workshops.

Workshop Topics Include:

- Practical Activities for Teaching Gifted Children
- Differentiating in the Regular Classroom
- How to Help Children Read, Write and Think Better
- Using <u>Stories with Holes</u> and Other Thinking Activities
- Powerful Strategies to Enhance Learning
- Communicating Better in the Workplace
- Communicating Better at Home
- Communicating Better at School
- The Principal as an Educational Leader
                     and many more...

Other Titles By Nathan Levy

Not Just Schoolwork
Volumes 1-4

Write, From the
Beginning
(*Revised Edition*)

Thinking and Writing
Activities for the Brain!
Books 1 and 2

Creativity Day-by-Day
(Stimulating Activities
for Kids and Adults)

Stories with Holes
Volumes 1-20

Intriguing Questions
Volumes 1-6

Whose Clues
Volumes 1-6

Nathan Levy's
Test Booklet of Basic
Knowledge for Every
American Over 9 Years
Old

There Are Those

101 Things Everyone
Should Know About
Science

Stories with Holes Gift Set Volumes 1-12

Sample stories taken from 19 of the 20 original volumes of Stories with Holes. Some of the more difficult stories have been omitted. The glossy covers make this set more appropriate as a gift.

Please write or call to receive our current catalog.
NL Associates, Inc.
P.O. Box 1199
Hightstown, NJ 08520-0399
(732) 656 - 7822
www.storieswithholes.com

23